A Picture Book of

WATER BIRDS

Written by Grace Mabie
Illustrated by Roseanna Pistolesi

Troll Associates

CORMORANT

Cormorants are very good swimmers.
They use their wings and webbed feet
to dive deep underwater to hunt for fish.
But this bird's feathers don't shed water.
After it finishes hunting, a cormorant has to
spread its wings out so they can dry in the sun.

Most cormorants live on islands or rocky sea
cliffs in very large groups called *colonies*. Both
males and females care for the 2–4 eggs and feed
the helpless, hungry chicks after they hatch.

Library of Congress Cataloging-in-Publication Data

Mabie, Grace, (date).
    A picture book of water birds / by Grace Mabie; illustrated by
Roseanna Pistolesi.
        p.   cm.
    Summary: Briefly introduces eighteen water birds, such as grebe,
cormorant, puffin, wandering albatross, and loon.
    ISBN 0-8167-2436-9 (lib. bdg.)   ISBN 0-8167-2437-7 (pbk.)
    1. Water birds—Juvenile literature.   [1. Water birds.
2. Birds.]   I. Pistolesi, Roseanna, ill.   II. Title.
QL676.2.M32   1992
598.29 '24—dc20   91-34129

CANADA GOOSE

You may have seen these handsome birds swimming in a park, or heard them honking as they fly overhead at night or early in the morning. Canada geese are quite at home around people. You might even see a few looking for food in people's yards!

Canada geese pair for life. They make their nests out of sticks and grass. It takes about a month for the eggs to hatch. A few days after they are born, the chicks can swim. But it will be about 2 months before the young *goslings* can fly.

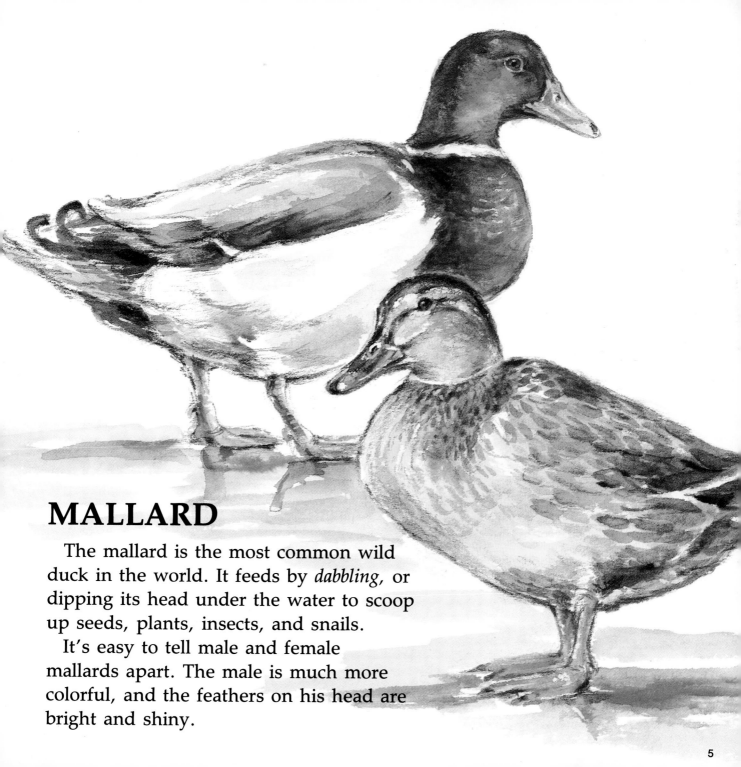

MALLARD

The mallard is the most common wild duck in the world. It feeds by *dabbling*, or dipping its head under the water to scoop up seeds, plants, insects, and snails.

It's easy to tell male and female mallards apart. The male is much more colorful, and the feathers on his head are bright and shiny.

KINGFISHER

Perched on a low branch, the kingfisher looks for fish in the water below. When it spots one, the bird dives into the water and quickly scoops the fish up with its pointed beak. It then tosses the fish in the air and swallows it headfirst.

Female kingfishers lay 5–7 eggs in the spring. After they hatch, the parents take turns feeding small fish to the chicks. Some young kingfishers can gobble up more than 15 fish a day!

ANHINGA

This bird is also called the *darter* or the *snakebird* because it swims with only its head and neck above water. As the anhinga (an-HIHNG-guh) swims underwater, its long, sharp beak spears fish and frogs. The anhinga comes to the surface to eat, tossing its prey up in the air and then swallowing it headfirst.

An anhinga's feathers don't shed water, as most other birds' do. So after it has been underwater, the anhinga has to perch on a branch or log and spread its wings out to dry.

GREBE

Have you ever seen a bird walk on water? Grebes sometimes do. Their feet move so fast that they can run across the surface of a lake or marsh, churning up water as they go.

It's hard for a grebe to walk on land. Its feet are so far back on its body, the grebe can't keep its balance. But grebes are so at home in the water that they even build their nests there. Both the male and the female pull up weeds and other plants to make a nest that floats on the water. The female lays 2–8 eggs in the nest. They hatch in 3–4 weeks.

For the first 2 weeks, the little chicks ride on their parents' backs. They even hang on when Mom and Dad dive underwater to catch a fish or some insects for dinner!

WHOOPING CRANE

The tallest bird in North America, the whooping crane stands 4–5 feet (1.2–1.5 meters) tall and has a wing-span of 6–8 feet (1.8–2.4 meters). That's a big bird!

Whooping cranes get their name from the loud, trumpetlike cry they make. These calls are how the birds "talk" to each other.

AVOCET

The long-legged avocet (AV-uh-seht) is a type of *wading bird*. It wades through shallow water in lakes, ponds, and marshes, looking for food. The avocet moves its bill through the water, or scrapes it along the bottom, to catch insects and small water animals.

Groups of avocets nest in the mud or sand at the water's edge. Here, the females lay about 4 eggs.

GREEN-BACKED HERON

Like many birds that live near water, green-backed herons like to eat fish and other water animals. This bird will stand very still for a long time, staring into the water. When it spots a fish, the heron strikes. Its head darts forward, and its long, sharp bill grabs a tasty snack. Green-backed herons that live in zoos have even been known to use bait to catch fish! They will drop some food into the water, then wait patiently until their *prey* comes close enough to catch.

Herons hunt alone, but they live in large colonies. They usually build their nests in trees or bushes. It takes about a month and a half for young chicks to hatch from the 2–7 eggs each female lays.

FLAMINGO

Flamingos are very easy birds to spot. With their long, thin legs and long necks, these tall, colorful birds really stand out in a crowd!

A flamingo feeds by holding its bill upside-down and sucking up water and mud. A special part of the flamingo's bill takes tiny plants called *algae* out of the water. They eat the algae and squirt out the water. A chemical in the algae is what makes the flamingo's feathers pink or red.

Flamingos usually lay only one egg at a time. The chick is white at first, but turns gray in a few days. It is only when it is about a year and a half old that the young bird gets its colorful adult feathers.

GANNET

These birds hunt by diving into the water and grabbing fish on their way back to the surface. Gannets are so at home in the water that they even sleep there. The only time they come on land is to build nests on cliffs near the sea. The females usually lay only one egg at a time. Both parents take turns feeding the chick for about 2 months. Then the young gannet can take care of itself.

WANDERING ALBATROSS

Albatrosses spend most of their lives flying over the ocean. They can glide on the wind for hours, hardly ever flapping their wings.

Large colonies of albatrosses usually nest on islands. Couples pair for life. About every other year, the female lays one egg. It takes almost 3 months for the chick to hatch. And it is nearly a year before the young albatross is ready to go out on its own.

LOON

Loons can dive deeper and stay underwater longer than any other bird. Their feet and wings help them swim quickly. A loon's body is well-suited to the water, but it is very clumsy on land. So a loon spends most of its time in water.

Loons usually lay 2 eggs. Chicks can swim as soon as they are born. But for the first 2 weeks, the chicks often ride on their parents' backs. Here they are safe and warm.

COMMON EIDER

The eider (EYE–duhr) is a kind of sea duck. It is one of the largest ducks. Eiders are covered with soft, thick feathers called *down*. This helps the ducks keep warm in the cold seas of the far north, where they live. Down keeps people warm, too. It is used to make quilts, pillows, and sleeping bags.

MUTE SWAN

The mute swan got its name because it is much quieter than most swans. It does not whistle or call. It can only make hissing or snorting noises.

Swans are related to ducks and geese. A swan's long neck helps it reach plants that grow deep under the water. And swans are good at both swimming and flying. They make a big splash when they come in for a landing!

MURRE

Huge colonies of murres (MURS) nest together on rocky cliffs near the northern seas. The large number of birds in a colony helps protect the eggs. So many murres nest together that it is impossible for enemies to get close enough to snatch the eggs away.

A murre does not build a nest, but lays her egg on bare rock. Different birds lay different-colored eggs. This helps the parents spot their own egg in the crowd.

RED PHALAROPE

Phalaropes (FAL-uh-rohps) have an interesting way of catching food. They swim in circles, paddling quickly with their feet. This churns up the water and brings insects and other animals to the surface for the phalarope to eat.

These birds are very good swimmers. A layer of trapped air under their feathers helps them float lightly on top of the water. Phalaropes are so light that a strong wind can pick one up off the water and carry it miles away!

PUFFIN

This bird looks so much like a parrot that it is sometimes called a *sea parrot*. But parrots and puffins are not related.

Puffins live in the cold northern oceans. They are very good swimmers and divers, and feed mostly on fish. In June and July, they lay their eggs on islands or rocky cliffs. The parents take care of their single chick for about 2 months.